THE AUTHOR

Paolo Crippa (23 April 1978) has cultivated his passion for Italian history since high school. His research interests are focused mainly in the field of military history and in particular on italian armored units from the 30s until the end of World War II. In 2006 he published his first volume, "I Reparti Corazzati della Repubblica Sociale Italiana 1943/1945", the first organic research carried out and published in Italy on the subject. In 2007 he published "Duecento Volti della R.S.I." and in 2011 " Un anno con il 27° Reggimento Artiglieria Legnano". He regularly contributes to several journals: Milites, New Historica, SGM - World War II, Batailes & Blindes, Armoured Vehicles and history of the twentieth century, Mezzi Corazzati, both as an author, or in collaboration with other researchers. He published with the editor Mattioli 1885 in 2014 "Italy 43 – 45 – Civil War improvised AFV's" (2014), "Italian AFV's of the Civil War 1943 - 1945" (2015) and "Italy 43 – 45 – AFV's and MV's of co-belligerent units" (2018).

Carlo Cucut was born in Nole (TO) in 1955. He cultivated a passion for history as a boy and over the years has deepened this interest by dedicating himself to historical research. He published articles in the italian magazines: "Storia del XX Secolo", "Storie & Battaglie", "Milites" and "Ritterkreuz". He published various volumes for Marvia Edizioni: "Penne Nere on the eastern border. History of the Alpini's Regiment "Tagliamento" 1943-1945 ", winner of the "De Cia" Award; "Attilio Viziano. Memories of a war correspondent "; "Armed Forces of RSI on the eastern front"; "Armed Forces of RSI on the Western Front"; "Armed Forces of RSI on the Gothic Line"; "Alpini in the City of Rijeka 1944-1945". For the Trentino Modeling Group he published "The armed forces of RSI 1943-1945. Land forces ".

PUBLISHING'S NOTES

None of unpublished images or text of our book may be reproduced in any format without the expressed written permission of Luca Cristini Editore (already Soldiershop.com) when not indicate as marked with license creative commons 3.0 or 4.0. Luca Cristini Editore has made every reasonable effort to locate, contact and acknowledge rights holders and to correctly apply terms and conditions to Content.

Every effort has been made to trace the copyright of all the photographs. If there are unintentional omissions, please contact the publisher in writing at: info@soldiershop.com, who will correct all subsequent editions.

Our trademark: Luca Cristini Editore©, and the names of our series & brand: Soldiershop, Witness to war, Museum book, Bookmoon, Soldiers&Weapons, Battlefield, War in colour, Historical Biographies, Darwin's view, Fabula, Altrastoria, Italia Storica Ebook, Witness To History, Soldiers, Weapons & Uniforms, Storia etc. are herein © by Luca Cristini Editore.

LICENSES COMMONS

This book may utilize part of material marked with license creative commons 3.0 or 4.0 (CC BY 4.0), (CC BY-ND 4.0), (CC BY-SA 4.0) or (CC0 1.0). We give appropriate attribution credit and indicate if change were made in the acknowledgments field. Our WTW books series utilize only fonts licensed under the SIL Open Font License or other free use license.

ACKNOWLEDGMENTS

A Special Thanks from the authors to: Archivio Monterosa, Arch. Viziano, Arch. Crippa, Arch. Reduci Reggimento "Tagliamento", Arch. Quaquaro, Arch. Galliani, Arch. Cucut, Arch. Comin, Arch. Dini, Arch. Panzarasa, Arch. Roberti, Arch. Crivellari. For all the titles of our serie we tanks also US national archives NARA, US Library of Congress, Bundesarchiv/wikipedia, Kriegsberichter archiv and Polish national archives. Thanks to the Europeana Collections, and at all the several institution, museum, library, bibliotecks, public or private collection & athenaeums that with their positive copyright policy about part of his collections, allows us the use of many images present in our books. We remember same of this great World Institutions: New York Public Library, Rara CH, Heidelberg Biblioteck University, Rijkmuseum of Amsterdam, Dusseldorf University Library, Polona Library, Herzog August Bibliothek of Wolfenbüttel, Stuttgart Bibliothek, SLUB Dresden, Frankfurt am Main Universitätsbibliothek, Europeana, Wikipedia, and many others...

For a complete list of Soldiershop titles please contact Luca Cristini Editore on our website: www.soldiershop.com or www.cristinieditore.com.
E-mail: info@soldiershop.com

Title: **BERSAGLIERI'S UNITS OF THE ITALIAN SOCIAL REPUBLIC**   Code.: **WTW-005 EN**
By Carlo Cucut and Paolo Crippa. Cover colored images by Roberto Costanzo (Ro Color) and Anna Cristini
ISBN code: 978-88-93274777 First edition, July 2019
Language: English, Nr. of photos: 117, size: 177,8x254mm Cover & Art Design: Luca S. Cristini

WITNESS TO WAR (SOLDIERSHOP) is a trademark of Luca Cristini Editore, via Orio, 35/4 - 24050 Zanica (BG) ITALY.

WITNESS TO WAR

BERSAGLIERI'S UNITS OF THE ITALIAN SOCIAL REPUBLIC

PHOTOS & IMAGES FROM WORLD WARTIME ARCHIVES

CARLO CUCUT - PAOLO CRIPPA

SUMMARY:

1st Bersaglieri Division "Italia"..5

2nd Division Granatieri "Littorio" – II Exploring Battalion..10

4th Alpini's Division "Monterosa" – Exploring Group "Cadelo"..10

III Bersaglieri Battalion "Natisone" - Alpini Regiment "Tagliamento"...................................11

3rd Bersaglieri Regiment..16

CI Battalion Complements Bersaglieri..17

I (LI) Coastal Defense Volunteer Bersaglieri Battalion...17

II (XX) Coastal Defense Volunteer Bersaglieri Battalion..18

III (XXV) Coastal Defense Volunteer Bersaglieri Battalion..20

IV (XVIII) Coastal Defense Volunteer Bersaglieri Battalion...20

1st Regiment "Bersaglieri di Marcia"..21

Bersaglieri Volunteer Regiment "Luciano Manara"..21

1st Bersaglieri Volunteer Battalion "Benito Mussolini" – XV Coastal Defense Battalion........22

2nd Bersaglieri Volunteer Battalion "Goffredo Mameli"..24

3rd Volunteers Battalion Bersaglieri "Enrico Toti"..25

1st Company "Bersaglieri del Mincio" – Raggruppamento "Cacciatori degli Appennini"........25

1st Battalion Arditi Bersaglieri – Raggruppamento Anti Partigiani....................................25

Other units...26

1st Battalion of Italian Volunteer "Ettore Muti" 26

Compagnia Bersaglieri "Curzio Casalecchi" – Legione Autonoma Mobile "Ettore Muti".......26

"Fulmine" Battalion – "Decima" Division...26

Photos..27

Bibliography...99

BERSAGLIERI UNITS OF R.S.I.

The general disarray caused by the Armistice on 8 September also had immediate repercussions on the Bersaglieri's units, both present in the Peninsula and abroad. The Bersaglieri, however, were among the first to reorganize and take up arms again, both in the South, where at the end of September 1943 the LI Battalion of Bersaglieri was included in the First Motorized Group, and in the North. In the territory of what would later be the Italian Social Republic, the first non-politicized department to take up arms again alongside the Germanic Ally was the Bersaglieri Battalion "Mussolini", which began re-establishing itself in Verona on 11st September in the barracks of the 8th Bersaglieri Regiment, nucleus of what would later be the "Luciano Manara" Bersaglieri Regiment. In Milan, the 3rd Volunteer Regiment was formed, with personnel from the Regio Esercito Regiment of the same name, and during the following weeks four Battalions, XVIII, XX, XXV and LI were formed. At the beginning of 1944 the Regiment Command was moved to Germany to reach the "Italia" Bersaglieri Division in constitution and the battalions that formed it became autonomous, changing the numbering. The "Italia" Bersaglieri Division was established in Heuberg in Germany with volunteers from the concentration camps and was then deployed south of Parma, fought in Garfagnana and disbanded on April 28th in Val di Taro. Outside the national territory we remember the events of the Bersaglieri Battalion "Zara", emblematic of that terrible moment of passage, caused by September 8th. Displaced since 1941 in the area of the redeemed city, in fact isolated from the rest of the Kingdom of Italy, the Bersaglieri Zara Battalion had participated, together with other Italian and German units, in continuous containment actions. At the time of the Armistice, the Battalion, which was stationed as a garrison in the town of Biograd (Zaravechia), fell back on Zara, where the officers found themselves faced with a dilemma: to collaborate with the Germans or end up in prison camps, given that it was impossible to attempt a resistance against the Germanic armed forces. A compromise was reached: the Italians would remain as garrison of the city, to defend it above all against the reaction and the annexation ambitions of the Croatian Ustashas. The Battalion thus dedicated itself to this exhausting garrison activity, but, with a slow but inexorable haemorrhage, the city's units gradually lost men, some of them sent in Germany, others escaped among the partisans or fleeing to their homes in Venezia Giulia. After the first terrible Allied bombing in the autumn of 1943, what remained of the battalion, about 200 men, was transferred to Trieste to become part of the army of the R.S.I. January 4th, 1944. Some Bersaglieri wanted to stay and, disarmed by the Germans, they were sent to various neighboring localities to be employed as labor-power.

1st Bersaglieri Division "Italia"

The "Italia" Bersaglieri Division was officially established in November 1943, but only in the spring of 1944 it begun its training in the Heuberg Camp in Pomerania. It was made up of former internees, conscripts and volunteers from the Great Unit Constitution Center. Completed the training period, on 17th July 1944 it marched in front of the Duce, receiving, at the end of the parade, the combat flags for its Regiments. It seemed therefore that the time of the return of "Italy" to its homeland had come but, due to the controversy that broke out with the Germans about the sending of thousands of Italian soldiers to Germany to be incorporated into the Flak and the withdrawal of the German armament destined for the constitutions German divisions to be sent to the western front, the Division's final training was blocked, to resume in August and ended in the fall. It was therefore only in the month of December 1944 that the Division was able to return to Italy, with a transfer made particularly difficult by the lack of means of transport and by the aerial bombardments of the railway lines which, causing multiple interruptions, forced many Units to finish the journey for railway to Brescia or Verona, and to complete the transfer on foot to the Division's concentration area, located between Parma, Sala Baganza (PR) and Pontremoli (MS). The transfers on foot were carried out during the night, to avoid air strikes, with stretches of even 50 kilometers in length, in extremely critical weather conditions, caused by heavy rain and snow. Once in the assigned area, the Divisional Command was placed in Ozzano (BO), the 1st Bersaglieri Regiment in Berceto (PR), the 2nd Bersaglieri Regiment in the North West of Collecchio (PR), east of the Taro River, the 4th Regiment Artillery between Collecchio and Ozzano, the 4th Exploring Group in Sala Baganza, the Tank Hunters in Fornovo (PR), the Services and the Intendancy in Felino (PR) and Sala Baganza. The fatigue of the transfer, the conditions of the clothing, the situation of dispersion in so many nucleuses, favored the propaganda of the civilians and of the partisans who incited to the desertion, beyond to loosen the discipline. In the early days of January 1945, the German Command began the Operation "Totila", a vast anti-partisan round-up in the mountain area in the Parma area between Borgo Val di Taro, Bardi, Bedonius, and the rear of Aulla. The Bersaglieri of the 2nd Regiment of the "Italy" Division also participated in the roundup. Towards the middle of January 1945 the transfer of the "Italy" to the line of the Serchio Valley began, through the Passo della Cisa, Pontremoli and Aulla, a transfer that was carried out especially at night to avoid the Allied air offense, made even more arduous and tiring due to the lack of means of transport and the prohibitive weather conditions, with heavy snowfalls that delayed the arrival on the line. However, there were many divisions in the Division that remained in the Parma area, from military hospitals to divisional warehouses, from the garrisons intended for the control of the route S.S. 62 of the Cisa to those intended for the protection of the Parma - Pontremoli railway line. Only towards the end of January began the exchange of deliveries between the Commands. On the Garfagnana's front, the units of "Italia" replaced the "Monterosa", "San Marco" and 148. German Infanteriedivision units. The sector of the Apuan Alps and the Serchio Valley thus became the responsibility of the "Italia", to which the "Intra" Battalion and the "Bergamo" Artillery Group of the "Monterosa" remained, with the task of helping the insertion of the Bersaglieri in line, very tried and discouraged joints at the front. Between the 24th and 26th of January, the Division was visited by the Duce, who wanted to see for himself the state of the Bersaglieri and try to lift the morale of the soldiers. In addition to the Ozzano Division Headquarters, Mussolini also visited some principals, inspected the departments of the Collecchio area, in Pontremoli and near Aulla, and then returned to Gargnano. From 4th to 11th February the Americans launched Operation "Fourth Term", with a diversionary attack in the Serchio Valley and the main attack in the coastal sector of Versilia, with the aim of overcoming the coastal resistance line and reaching Massa, thus disrupting the Massa Rigel which prevented it from reaching the La Spezia stronghold. This was the first real test of fire for the Bersaglieri of the "Italia", even if only one sector was of their competence, as the line was still defended by Alpini and Marò joined the new arrivals to gain experience. At the end of the American offensive the positions remained practically unchanged, but this thanks to the veterans of the "Monterosa" and the "San Marco" who contributed, with the German and Italian reserve units, to restore the leaks that were opened due to the collapse of some departments of the 2nd Battalion of the 1st Regiment, collapse caused by the inexperience of war of the Bersaglieri and the poor quality of some officers. Having passed this test and completed the replacement with the previous on-line departments, the Bersaglieri of "Italia" provided good evidence, demonstrating their quality and recovering confidence in their means during the subsequent stay at the front. The Divisional Command was deployed to Camporgiano, formerly the headquarters of the previous "Monterosa" Command, while, starting from 21st February, General Carloni summarized the Division Command. When the Allied final offensive began in April 1945, the Division remained firmly established on its positions despite having its sides uncovered, due to the retreat of the German Divisions which were forced to yield to the pressure of the Allied troops. From April 10th, a series of interventions were arranged between General Carloni and General Fretter-Pico, commander of the 148. Infanteriedivision, whose goal was the withdrawal of the units towards the bank of the Po through the Passo del Cerreto, to Reggio Emilia, and through the Passo della Cisa to Parma, also collecting the units coming from La Spezia. To safely carry out this folding, a series of defensive strongholds were set up with the task of stopping the Allied avant-garde advancing along the coast and towards the hinterland behind the Serchio Valley. Two Combat Groups were therefore established, called "Gruppo Ferrario" and "Gruppo Zelli-Jacobuzzi" from the name of the respective Commanders, who had the task of acting as rearguard, to delay as much as possible the advance of the Allies. The fall back towards the Po Valley was heavily opposed by continuous bombardments, which caused heavy losses in men, vehicles, quadrupeds and wagons, and in some areas the partisans made their appearance by sniping. But the action of the Fighting Groups was particularly harsh, as they opposed the Allied attacks as long as they had strength. The fights sustained on the Colle Musatello and on the quotas of Viano are remarkable, where on the 22nd the 1st Company of the "Mameli" Battalion, of the "Ferrario Group", and of San Terenzo and Ceserano from the "Zelli-Jacobuzzi Group" were decimated. The wards were concentrated at Fornovo Taro, the last fight took place on the 28th, with the "Ferrario Group" that tried to overcome the Taro to break through the Allied lines and continue the retreat, an attempt rejected by the preponderant opposing forces. On April 29th, 1945, the "Italia" Division surrendered to the Brazilians of the F.E.B. receiving the honor of arms.

Divisional Structure
- Commander: General of Giardina Division, then Colonel i.g.s. Mario Carloni, then Colonel i.g.s. Guido Manardi (Brigadier General since 19th August 1944), and finally Brigade General (Division General since 22 February 1945) Mario Carloni.
- Officer Officers: Lieutenant Martella, Lieutenant Valli, Lieutenant Henzel.
- Office 1 / A Operations: Commander Lieutenant Colonel Teodoro Anela, then Colonel Luigi Tarsia, finally Lieutenant Colonel Antonio Bertone.
- Officer Officers: Captain Ferrari, Lieutenant Travaglia.
- Office 1 / B Services: Captain Captain i.g.s. Tescion,; officers Captain Peradotto.
- Office 1 / C Information: Captain pensive, Captain Loffredo, Captain Ruisi.
- Officer Officers: Tenente Cambiè, Lieutenant Citizens, Lieutenant Ulivieri, Lieutenant Vaccari, Lieutenant Bonato, Lieutenant Pilotti.
- Office 1 / D Training: Lieutenant Verderoni.
- Office 2 / A Personnel: Captain Salinari, Maggiore DAutilia.
- Office 2 / B Staff: Lieutenant Fragiacomo.
- Court: Commander Lieutenant Colonel Spitaleri, officers Lieutenant Faranda, Captain Pasquinangeli, Lieutenant Muder, Lieutenant Nocentini.
- Office 4 / A Intendenza: commander Major Pacini, officers Captain Pierallini, Lieutenant Giaccone, Lieutenant Roncarolo.
- Office 4 / B Health: Major Ferrari Doctor.
- Office 4 / C Veterinary: Commander Captain Veterinary Da Como-Annoni, officers Bardi Lieutenant.
- Office 4 / D Spiritual Assistance: Captain Enrico Don Saporiti.
- Office 5 Transportation: Captain Gherardi.
- Deposit: commander Colonel Casanova, then Colonel Arpaja, officers Captain Nigrelli, Major De Silva, Captain Lo Monaco.
- Interpreters group: Lieutenant Iselghio, Lieutenant Nascinbeni.
- Gendarmerie: Captain Piciocchi.
- 4th GNR Section: Lieutenant Menga.
- 7th GNR Section: Lieutenant Beretta.
- UDOF: Captain F. Bologna, Lieutenant Muner, Lieutenant Bracciolini.
- D.K.V. n. 180: General Oetchen, then General Eibl.

1st Bersaglieri Regiment
- Regimental Command Company
- Light Column

- I Battalion
- II Battalion
- III Battalion
-   107th Tank Hunters Company

2nd Bersaglieri Regiment
- Regimental Command Company
- Light Column
- I Battalion
- II Battalion
- III Battalion
- 108th Tank Hunters Company

4th Artillery Regiment
- Regimental Command Battery
- Light Column
- I 75/13 Howitzers Group (on Group Command Battery e 3 Batteries)
- II 75/27 Guns Group (on Group Command Battery e 2 Batteries)[1]
- III 149/19 Howitzers Heavy Group (on Group Command Battery e 3 Batteries)
- IV Group (o Group Command Battery e 2 Batteries)[2]

IV Exploring Group
Command Unit

- 1st Light Squadron
- 2nd Light Squadron
- 3rd Heavy Squadron

Divisional Units
- IV Pioneers Battalion
- IV Battalion Connections
- IV Transport Battalion (5 transport columns and 1 warehouse)
- CIV Complements Battalion (kept in a square position)
- 4th Divisional Anti-tank Company

Health Department on:
o   104th Healthcare Company
o   4th Healthcare Company
o   IV Surgical Core
o   IV Ambulances Platoon

Administration Unit on:
o   Administration Company
o   Bakers Company
o   Butchers Company
o   Veterinary Company
o   Workshop Company
o   Subsistence Company

4th e 7th G.N.R.'s Sections
Military Tribunal
Divisional Deposit

---

1   The Group II arrived in Italy was equipped with 75/18 howitzers to replace the 75/27 guns, but they were so badly used that the Command was undecided whether to keep the old 75/27 in service.

2   The IV Artillery Group, following the reorganization of the Division in the last part of the training in Germany, was not used as such, but provided its staff to the other three Groups of the 4th Artillery Regiment and was disbanded.

Staff

In June 1944 a document reported a total of 14,183 soldiers, of which 3,720 former military prisoners, 9,902 flowed from Italy and 561 already in the area. At the 1st of September 1944 the new armament tables included: 461 officers, 1,864 non-commissioned officers and 9,047 troops, for a total of 11,367 military personnel, while the real situation presented a Division force of 11,960 men, with a surplus of officers and NCOs. The organic situation on February 28th, 1945 shows a table with a total of 10,962 Italians and 1,237 Germans including officers, non-commissioned officers, troops, interpreters and civil personnel, and a staff of 8,831 Italians and 1,188 Germans.

Weapons

The individual and divisional armament was a mixture of German and Italian material, there were Mauser 98k and model 91, Breda 30 light machine guns, MG42 and Breda 37 heavy machine guns, the guns were Italian and German. The mortars were 81 mm Italian and 80 mm German. The situation with regard to the supply of cannons and howitzers was very difficult. The Artillery Groups were equipped with 75/27 guns, 75/13 Italian howitzers and 149/19; at the arrival in Italy the 75/27 guns were replaced with 75/18 howitzers. In the weapons tables there were also 10 guns 7.5 IG18, 4 guns 15 SIG35 and 17 guns 7.5 Pak 40. In reality, on January 25th, 1945, the Division Commander complained of the presence of a single piece of 15, the lack of light infantry guns, replaced by 3 cannons of 65/17 without means of pointing, therefore useless, leftovers of 1st World War, while it did not mention the presence of the anti-tanks. It should be noted that the 149/19 howitzers of the III Group, were withdrawn a few days before reaching the line, when they were tried it was noticed that they were without liquid in the hydraulic recoil brakes, they had to spend many days before being able to make the pieces working . Panzerfausts were also included.

Vehicles

The "Italia" Division was the one that suffered the most from vehicle shortages, only the II Battalion / 1st Regiment was motorized, even the quadrupeds were largely insufficient.

The situation on January 25th, 1945 was as follows:

Vehicles : in organic 676, actually present 123 (deficiency 553)
Quadrupeds[3]: foreseen 4,104, actually present 1,281 (deficiency 2,720)
Carts : foreseen 603, actually present 142 (deficiency 461)

As of February 28th, the situation of quadrupeds was as follows:
foreseen 4,684, actually present 1,823 (deficiency 2,861)

For the quadrupeds the situation was serious not only for the shortage that varied between 60 and 70%, but also for the characteristics of the animals, both the horses and the mules were of small size and unsuitable for towing of heavy loads. This fact also stemmed from the decision of the Germans who, before the division returned from Germany, recovered 416 draft horses to be assigned to their units in formation, trusting in the reintegration of the staff once they arrived in Italy.

Particularly serious was the situation of the tractors for howitzers of the III Group of Artillery, instead of the Breda they had been assigned to the old Pavesi P4, absolutely unsuitable for their scarce reach and for little efficiency[4].

The shortage of trucks was very serious, out of 225 in the workforce there were 31, of which half inefficient. The considerable number of vehicles out of use was motivated by the total lack of workshops, none of the 12 planned was present.

Losse

They have been identified 481 deads, of which 19 are unknown, and 21 were shot for desertion or theft, among these 3 are unknown. These are Fallen on the front of the Garfagnana and in other areas where the departments of the Division have operated or stopped.

---

3 The quadrupeds also include the mules for the group with a certain number of staff which totaled 377 but in reality were 118.
4 Some witnesses instead indicate the presence of Breda tractors on the front, it is possible that these were supplied shortly before the transfer of the III Group online..

2nd Division Granatieri "Littorio" – II Exploring Battalion

The II Exploring Battalion was located between Val Pellice and Val Chisone, carrying out defense and security operations in the rear against the partisans, at the end of April 1945 it followed the Divisional Command, surrendering on 5th May 1945 in the "Zona franca"of Strambino Romano. The first commander of the Battalion was Captain Fabio Galigani, later replaced by Captain Nello Presico, and finally by Captain Anco Marzio Da Pas.
Structure:
- Command
- Command Department
- 1st light squadron
- 2nd light squadron
- 3rd heavy squadron

4th Alpini's Division "Monterosa" – Exploring Group "Cadelo"

The Exploring Group was established in Vercelli, in January 1944, with Bersaglieri from the 4th Regiment of Turin and the 5th Regiment of Siena as the XXIII Exploring Group "Fiamme Cremisi". In the same month it was placed in the 4th Alpine Division "Monterosa", as an exploring unit, then transferred to Germany where it trained in the Feldstet field. Returning to Italy at the end of July, it was relocated to Borzonasca with the functions of divisional reserve. At the end of August, it took part in the great operation for the safety of the communication routes behind the anti-boarding deployment. Starting from Borzonasca it moved towards Rezzoaglio and arrived in Santo Stefano d'Aveto on the 28th, after some fighting against the partisan forces and the overcoming of considerable road interruptions, capturing a considerable amount of weapons and vehicles. After this operation IT remained As a garrison in the Val d'Aveto, based in Rezzoaglio and at the end of September it detached a Platoon at Passo del Bocco. On September 27th, in Santo Stefano d'Aveto, with the classic partisan ambush, Major Cadelo, commander of the Group, was killed and in his honor the Exploring Group took his name: "Cadelo Exploring Group". In early November, following the passage of much of the "Vestone" Battalion to the partisans, it carried out round-ups in the Barbagelata area, recovering Alpini, weapons, ammunition and quadrupeds. At the end of October it was transferred to the Garfagnana front where, from 2nd November, having arrived in Piazza al Serchio, it was assigned to the divisional reserve function. But just two days later, on November 4th, it sent first a Platoon of the 2nd Squadron, then the whole Squadron and then moved there to the full. It was deployed to the west of the Serchio river in the sector: Sassi - Eglio - Monte Grottorotondo - Le Rocchette, joining the "Intra" Alpini Battalion and the Marò of the "Uccelli" Battalion of "San Marco" Division, on the Case Pozza-Case line Cornola, with the Potone Cannons, armed with four 75/10 cavalry pieces, placed at Eglio. Unfortunately, the defensive line was very rarefied, given that the positions, defended by 4 or 5 Bersaglieri, were two or three hundred meters away from each other. It actively participated in the defensive fighting following the American offensives of November, for the reconquest of the 832, 1029, 1031 and 1068 quotas reached by the Americans, therefore it counterattacked the enemy alignment with patrols in depth. At the end of November, the 2nd Squadron suffered some partisan attacks, which led to the capture of many Bersaglieri and the loss of some positions. The technique adopted was always the same: partisans disguised as Bersaglieri or Alpini approached the positions and as soon as they entered they made the soldiers prisoners. Following the retrieval of a correspondence from a partisan brigade, the names of four officers of the "Cadelo" who were in contact with the partisans were in possession: three were captured and one managed to escape. From that moment the attacks against the men of the "Cadelo" ended. In December it actively participated in the failure of the offensive, launched on the 12th by the Americans of the 92nd "Buffalo" Division with the support of the partisans working behind the defenders, aiming to conquer the 832 quota. During the "Wintergewitter" offensive of the Christmas 1944, the "Cadelo" was destined to perform one of the four demonstration episodes foreseen by the plan of attack. Almost immediately occupied Calomini, it bypassed Vergemoli and, having crossed the Turrite di Gallicano, reached Fornovolasco and Trassilico, thus continuing with the activity of patrols deep within the enemy lines, in the Trombacco area. During these operations, a Platoon of Bersaglieri of the 1st Division "Italy" was aggregated to the "Cadelo", the first unit of this Division to reach the front. From the end of the Christmas offensive until February 1945, the "Cadelo" remained deployed in the positions set on the new defensive line. In early February it was replaced in line with the 3rd Battalion of the 1st Bersaglieri Regiment of the "Italy" Division, beginning the transfer to Liguria. On the way it was sent to support the German 148 Infanteriedivision, to reoccupy some positions in the Massa sector, and finally it arrived on February 23rd in Liguria, placing the Command and two Squadrons between Terrarossa and Borgonuovo and the other Squadron in Sestri Levante. In mid-March it made a round-up in the hinterland towards the Apennine Passes. On April 24th, the "Cadelo" met in Chiavari with the other unis of "Monterosa", under the command of Colonel Pasquali, and began its retreat towards the Po, which was linked to them. On April 25th, 26th and 27th it supported rearguard fights against the American avant-garde on Entella and Ruta. On 27th April, in the north of Uscio, it surrendered with the honor of arms.

Structure
- Command
- Command Squadron
- 1st Light Squadron
- 2nd Light Squadron
- 3rd Heavy Squadron
- Vehicles Unit

The 1st and 2nd Squadrons were composed of four Plotons, three light and one heavy; the light Plotons were composed of four Teams, each team had a LMG 42, a miter and a grenade launcher; the heavy Platoon was composed of two SMG 42 heavy machine guns and two 80 mm mortar teams. The 3rd Squadron consisted of an anti-tank Platoon, an accompanying guns Platoon and a pioneer Platoon. Each squadron had a strength of about 213 men.

Weapons

The 3rd heavy squadron was equipped by three 75/43 Pak 40 anti-tank guns and 4 75/10 German IG 18 howitzers. The other two Squadrons were equipped by heavy machine guns and read MG42 and 80 mm mortars. The individual weapons were those in service in the Alpine departments of the Division, namely Mauser 98K, Beretta guns 34, machine guns.

Vehicles

The Autodrappello supplied 20 Lancia ESARO trucks and various other unidentified vehicles.

Losses

The losses of the "Cadelo" Exploring Group add up to 42, although the list is certainly incomplete.

III Bersaglieri Battalion "Natisone" - Alpini Regiment "Tagliamento"

On September 17th, 1943, just nine days after the armistice, the Battalions Group "Tagliamento" was re-established in Udine under the orders of Consul Ermacora Zuliani, former commander of the 63rd Legion of M.V.S.N. and then of the Armored Legionary Regiment of the "M" Division "Centauro" with the rank of Colonel. Taking possession of the 8th Alpini Barracks, he was able to supply a Public Order Company and the essential services and, despite the proclamation of the "Adriatic Coast" by the Germans, succeeded in increasing the staff to a satisfactory extent and, at the end of October, with a staff of about 500, created garrisons outside the city of Udine.

With the influx of volunteers and conscripts, between the end of 1943 and the first months of 1944 the workforce expanded considerably, reaching 1,412 men by the end of February.

The official birth of the 3rd Bersaglieri "Natisone" Battalion on three Companies dates back to January 1st, 1944, although only the first Company was being formed at that time. On 22nd January 1944, following the new provisions issued by the Regimental Command, the deployment of the Bersaglieri Battalion at the Udine headquarters was confirmed and the number of the 9th Company was assigned to the company in service. At the end of January the Battalion had a staff of about 150 men. The first operational deployment of the Battalion took place on February 9th, when, following a heavy attack by the 30th Division of the IX Corpus of Yugoslavia at the garrison of the 2nd Company of the Arditi Battalion at Faedis, a group of 15 Bersaglieri remained to strengthen the garrison. Below we transcribe the memoirs of a Bersagliere concerning this deployment:

"*After the attack on Faedis of 09.02.1944, led by a substantial formation of the 30th Division of the IX Korpus, a dozen, more or less, among the Bersaglieri reinforcements to the men of the garrison, are suddenly*" slammed "*in detachment to Canal of Grivò. They are commanded by a clear figure of a recently deceased soldier: Sergeant Degano Sergio. And there is no need to add anything else. We walk carelessly into the narrow space, where, among a few houses almost covered by woods, the Grivò descends into the short plain in front of the houses of Faedis. We are few and our Commander, who has the habit of always giving the example, issues clear orders: no checks, no checkpoints, nothing at all. The population must be left in peace. During the day systematic checks of the territory by paths and ravines, up to the ridge that from Canebola to S. Antonio and Madonnina del Domm turns to Pedrosa and Valle, at night shifts between houses, in the woods to surprise anyone who wants to attack us by surprise and give the alarm to the positions surrounding Faedis in time. A child! The population is all with us.* "
(testimony of a Bersagliere from 9th Company)

On 12th February a group of 10 Bersaglieri with a non-commissioned officer were posted to the garrison of Nimis. On the 14th, following a new attack by Mongolian deserters at the Nimis garrison, the "Natisone" Battalion had its first Fallen: the Bersagliere Aldo Venezian. On February 15th the 10th Company was formed, the second of the Battalion. Between 25th and 27th, two other Bersaglieri died in Nimis due to an accidental shot from a firearm. In March, with the arrival of the volunteers and the reinforcements of the levers 1923, 1924 and 1925, the Battalion approached the definitive structure. Between the end of March and the month of May, the department implemented its definitive organization and defined the activity it would carry out until the end of the conflict. On April 3rd, 1944, the provision for the new organization on 3 Battalions, 1 Regimental Command Company and 1 Training Company was applied. On 11th April the unit assumed its official name: "Alpini Regiment Tagliemento". On 18th April it was deployed on the Prepotto - Saga - Tarvisio line; a month later the Regiment established itself in more advanced positions, entering the Baccia Valley, the Isonzo and the Vipacco. The activity was mainly that of guarding infrastructures such as bridges, tunnels, railways, viaducts, power grids, power stations, in addition to that of presence against the infiltrations of the Yugoslavian partisans, who aimed to occupy Italian territory and then claim their possession after the war ended. Thus began a long period of intense patrol and counter-guerrilla activity against Slavic and Italian partisans, with violent clashes. The month of April was also the month where the final organization of the "Natisone" Battalion was completed. On 3rd April it was decided that, within 48 hours, the Battalion would assume the new organization: 9th and 10th Bersaglieri Company, 8th Alpini Company, which remained in Udine to finish the training. The numbering of the companies, at the end of May, was finally modified as follows: 7th (ex 9th), 8th (ex 10th) Bersaglieri, 9th (ex 8th) Alpine. Following the order to establish the Prepotto - Saga - Tarvisio safety line with the Regiment, on 12th April 1944 the Battalion moved to the Cividale, carrying out the following deployment: Battalion Command in Cividale; 9th Company with the command at San Pietro al Natisone and branches at Azzida, Tiglio, Pulfero and Loch; 10th Company with the command in Cividale and branches in Sanguarzo and Ponte San Quirino.

On May 18th, 1944, in compliance with the order to settle on a more advanced line-up, the Battalion

received the order to move to the Valle d'Isonzo, taking on the following line up between May 20th and 22nd:
- Battalion Command: from Cividale he moved to Canale d'Isonzo
- 7th Bersaglieri Company: Company Command at Plava (1 officer and 50 troop men), detachments at Descla (1 officer and 39 troops) and at Km 31 (1 officer- men of 44 troops);
- 8th Bersaglieri Company: Company Command in Canale d'Isonzo (3 officers and 109 troops), detachments in Ronzina (1 officer and 42 troops) and in Salona (consistency is not known);
- 9th Alpine Company: Company Command in Volzana (2 officers and 49 troops), detachments in Diga di Sella (men of 31 troops) and in Doblari (1 officer and 40 troops).

The strength of the Battalion on this date is 10 officers, non-commissioned officers in unknown numbers, 404 troops.

During the transfer, one of the columns carrying the 7th and 8th Company was attacked in the section between Cighino and Sella di Sotto:

" …. At the first discharge the driver of the first motor vehicle, Sergent Luigi Venuti, later deceased, and two Bersaglieri were injured: the others left the truck, lurking and reacting to the fire. The other car was also attacked and so was the third one, whose staff was preparing to defend themselves on the ground to prevent the opponent from approaching the parked cars. Thus developed a violent clash in which a platoon of the 9th Company stationed in Sella di Sotto and a platoon of Bersaglieri of the "Benito Mussolini" Battalion participated, attracted by the shots. These departments came to a completed battle, as after 30 minutes of fire, the partisans withdrew from the struggle, retreating to the mountains. "

(from the Historical Journal of the Regiment)

The losses were 3 fallen, 2 missing and 9 injured.

The deployment of the 3rd Battalion, from the roadman's house at Km. 31 south of Plava to Volzana, at the gates of Tolmino, included all the middle course of the Isonzo, the deployment was immediately subjected to attacks in Doblari and Plava. On 26th June 1944 in Brillasse near Plava, a patrol was attacked by partisan formations, which retreated as soon as reinforcements arrived. On June 8th at 3 am, a partisan formation valued in a hundred men, attacked the garrison of Descla, where there were 4 non-commissioned officers and 30 Bersaglieri. After an hour of fighting the partisans withdrew with 2 dead and 10 wounded. Losses suffered: 2 injured bersaglieri. The Diary of the Military Chaplain also focuses on the combat of Descla:

"Three hundred partisans, with automatic weapons and mortars, from the Bainsizza, attack the thirty men and the four non-commissioned officers of the stronghold of Descla. After an hour of fighting they retire with many wounded, leaving two of their fallen comrades on the ground, two of our wounded."

(testimony of the Military Chaplain)

The stronghold at Km. 31, which due to its location and its duties of surveillance and security of the national road, on the outskirts of Salcano, suffered continuous disturbances with shots from the Sabotino and with close attacks, on the evening of 13th June was heavily attacked by numerous partisan forces. From the report of the Regimental Command to Marshal Graziani:

"On the evening of June 1th3, at 9 pm, the detachment of Km. 31, on the Tolmino - Gorizia roadway, is attacked by a strong partisan band, valued at about 350 men, armed with automatic weapons and mortars. The strength of the detachment was 1 officer, 3 non-commissioned officers and 32 troop men, under the command of Lieutenant Geraci. The partisans occupied positions dominating the provision, given that this is located on the valley floor. After five hours of fighting, full of alternating events, about half a company of Blackshirts and "SS", truck-mounted, came from Gorizia. However, the autocolonna was blocked by the partisans and threatened with circumvention. Lieutenant Geraci, then, with a bold sortie behind the attackers, made with a part of his men, managed to break the circle and establish contact with the columnist, returning to the provision with all its components. Immediately after, however, the partisans returned violently to the attack of the detachment. The fighting lasted fiercely until 4:00 pm the next day, when the partisans, due to the losses suffered by our mortar,

were forced to retreat in disorder. Combat balance sheet:
on our part: 4 wounded
on the partisan side: 6 dead; 12 injured."

On June 14th, in a patrol action, Corporal Fogolin falls in Zagomila, a boarder captured during the battle manages to escape and returns to the garrison of Km. 31. During the night substantial partisan groups attack Auzza and Canale d'Isonzo. From the Historical Diary:

"June 14th, 1944 - Last night, partisan elements blew up the rolling stock in the Descla - Gorizia section at various points. The same night, from 11 pm to 6:30 am, large partisan forces attacked the garrison of Auzza which was overwhelmed and blew up the railway bridge. A patrol of ours (N.ote of the Author: of Bersaglieri da Ronzina under the command of Sergeant Antonio Dessena) rushed to desperate appeals: Sergeant Dessena Antonio and the bersagliere Urbani Cesare died following mortar shells. The same night, at 24, the detachment of Canale d'Isonzo was attacked frontally by important partisan forces which, divided into three groups, began a large fire of heavy and light automatic weapons. The fire of the garrison provoked a fight that ended at 2.30 pm with the flight of the attackers. The action was killed by the Bersagliere Maurano Antonio, born in 1927, who fell to the cry of "Viva l'Italia". Two other Bersaglieri were slightly injured. The partisan losses must have been significant to judge the clues found later. The behavior of the Bersaglieri was excellent, the high morale."

The following day the Historical Diary returns to the Canale attack with a clarification:

"... A brigade of three Battalions, with a total force of 300 men. The partisans suffered significant losses, ascertained in 7 deaths including the brigade commander. "

With regard to the attack on the Auzza garrison, a railway tollgate that has the task of defending the vital railway bridge on the Gorizia - Piedicolle - Klagenfurt line, defended by the soldiers of the XIV Coastal Defense Battalion, we transcribe excerpts from a Bersagliere report of the 8th Company that participated in the combat, posted to the stronghold of Ronzina:

"... There will be 400 meters in the air from Ronzina's detachment. The shots increase in intensity, as the night gets darker: it is a sign that also this time the IX Corpus partisans are going to get serious. It is also clear that the attacking partisan formations must be numerous. The alarm went off, and everyone is in the positions: we have the task of maintaining the viability on the Isonzo road Gorizia - Canale - Piedicolle, which is on the right bank of the Isonzo. The intensity of fire against the railway toll is continuously increasing. It is clear that the objective of the slave partisan forces is to blow up the railway bridge. The partisans launch flares, the mortar rounds follow each other continuously, while the machine-guns sing mournfully. The Costiero soldiers are perhaps a dozen, divided between the post on the bridge and those in the tollbooth, but respond to the fire with considerable boldness and great recklessness, even knowing that the ammunition supplied will not be able to last long. At one point, in fact, a Coastal soldier shows up at our stations to ask for ammunition, aware that they will have to withstand at least until the first light of day. Lieutenant Carandente, commander of Ronzina's Bersaglieri detachment, does not access the request, also because we are equipped with other machine guns. A patrol of volunteers is then formed to give reinforcement to the soldiers of Auzza: it is commanded by Sergeant Dessena, and includes Urbani, Zanet, two other bersaglieri and myself. The soldier precedes us, and we descend along the ridge on a zigzag path trying to hide in the sparse bushes. A flare illuminates us. The titini have sighted us and direct the mortar bombing towards our patrol. The sergeant gives us orders to distance ourselves, cover ourselves in the bushes, trying, each on his own, to reach the railway tollgate. I follow Dessena, then Urbani and Zanet, then the others. Immediately a mortar shot in our neighborhood, then two, then three. The Sergeant collapses at a bush. He urges me: "Go ahead!" I run along the slope. Travel across the suspension bridge over the Isonzo and reach the railway tollgate from the back. A soldier, with a leveled miter, realizes just in time that I am a Bersagliere, and asks me what I have come to do. He was right. I had some carbine magazines with me and a couple of hand grenades. Then I give an advice: "Go back, past the suspension bridge, don't go back along the path, but take to the right, that you will be more hidden by the trees." But I have to go over the suspension bridge, which is all open. I wait for a flare. I let it go out, and then with all my breath and energy I can retrace the bridge. Towards the end I stumble. I get up. The partisan machine guns continue to fire, and I jump with a jump into the woods. I've done

it! First of all, I find that I am unharmed and I breathe a sigh of relief; then I realize that I am alone. All I can do is reach my detachment. I climb. Arriving at a certain point on the road and running I reach our checkpoint, where Lieutenant Carandente is waiting for me. I ask where the other members of the patrol are and then, shouting in a frightened way, I say that Sergeant Dessena was injured, and we must go and get it. He replies that they have all returned, but the Urban Bersagliere is still missing. Meanwhile, the attack on the railway continues with increasing intensity. Heavy and light automatic weapons increase the volume of fire and at the toll station it is all a crackle, and a succession of tracers and mortar bursts. The soldiers respond with great audacity, throwing hand grenades beyond the tracks, where the partisans arrived. At 5:20 am a big explosion, almost a fireworks: the Slavic partisans managed to blow up the railway bridge of Auzza, after seven hours of hard fighting. A patrol of Bersaglieri of the detachment recovered, meanwhile, the bodies of Sergeant Antonio Dessena and Bersagliere Cesare Urbani."

(Major Capitain A.U. Lino Quaia)

During the months of August and September, the III "Natisone" Battalion was dissolved and its Companies were merged with the Regimental Command Company and the Command, this decision was taken due to the lack of staff. At the end of April the Regiment, with the Command, the C.C.R. and the I Battalion, moved to San Pietro al Natisone, where it was joined by the II Battalion, on April 30th the whole Regiment moved to Spignon, where it laid down its weapons.

Structure of Reggiment "Tagliamento"
- Compagnia Comando Reggimentale
- Gruppo Combattimento "Montenero"
- I Battaglione Alpini "Isonzo" su:
  - 1ª Compagnia
  - 2ª Compagnia
  - 3ª Compagnia
- II Battaglione Alpini "*Vipacco*" su:
  - 4ª Compagnia
  - 5ª Compagnia
  - 6ª Compagnia
- III Battaglione misto Bersaglieri e Alpini "Natisone" su:
  - 7ª Compagnia
  - 8ª Compagnia
  - 9ª Compagnia

Staff
- Compagnia Comando Reggimentale = 280 men
- Combat Group "*Montenero*" = 210/260 men
- I Battalion = 450 men
- II Battalion = 450 men
- III Battalion e = 450 men

In February 1944 the total number of active personnel was 1,412 military.
In March 1945 the total number of active personnel was 1,350 military.

Losses
Out of a total of around 2,000 men transiting the Regiment, there are 506 fallen, 69 missing, 45 slaughtered and over 600 wounded.

3rd Bersaglieri Regiment

The 3rd Bersaglieri Regiment was established in Milan immediately after 8th September, around Lieutenant Colonel Tarsia, who had not accepted the capitulation and moved to the command of M.V.S.N. of the town, agreeing to reconstitute the 3rd Regiment: on 27th September the Regiment was reborn. Lieutenant Colonel Tarsia's appeal was answered by many officers, non-commissioned officers and Bersaglieri who had not accepted the Armistice, in addition to soldiers of other units and numerous Lombard university students, who flocked to enlist. In a few weeks the Command, the Command Unit and 4 Battalions were established: the XX, the XVIII, the LI and the XXV. On 10th October 1943 Lieutenant Colonel Tarsia officially declared the 3rd Regiment reconstituted and 31st presented himself at the headquarters of the Republican Army to inform Marshal Graziani that the unit was ready for use at the front. At the end of November, by order of the German command (which does not like the employment of the Regiment at the front) the unit was transferred to the area of Alexandria, to continue the training and then be destined to coastal defense. On January 29th, 1944, in Tortona, and on the 30th, in Alexandria, after completing the training, the complete-rank Battalions take its oath. On February 15th, again following decisions taken by the German Commands, the Battalions of the 3rd Regiment become autonomous, change the numbering, and on the 20th they begin the transfer to Liguria, where they will be deployed on the coast with the task of coastal defense. The Command of the 3rd Regiment remains in Alexandria assuming the name "Inspectorate of Italian troops in Liguria". On March 30th, following the inclusion of the Bersaglieri Battalions in the larger German units deployed in Liguria, the Inspectorate was dissolved. Thus ended the history of the 3rd Bersaglieri Regiment[5].

Structure

Command (Milan, then Alessandria)
- Commander: Lieutenant Colonel Alfredo Tarsia
- Major Assistant: Captain Giuseppe Fadigati
- Officers: Captain Edoardo Penzo, Captain Pignolini, Medical Lieutenant Ugo Broglia, Lieutenant Giuseppe Petrone
- Chaplain Officer: Lieutenant Sante Don Bordignon
- Regimental Command Department (Captain Edoardo Penzo)
- Regimental Depot (Captain Vittorio De Bonis)

I Battalion (later number LI):
- Command Company
- 1st Company
- 2nd Company
- 3rd Company
- 4th Company

II Battalion (XX) on:
- Command Company
- 5th Company
- 6th Company
- 7th Company
- 8th Company
- 9th Company

III Battalion (XXV) on:
- Command Company
- 9th Company
- 10th Company
- 11th Company
- 12th Company

---

[5] Colonel Tarsia and some of his collaborators formed a Command at the disposal of the Vercelli Center for the establishment of the Great Units, with the task of organizing a Bersaglieri marching regiment to be included in the "Italy" Division.

IV Battalion (XVIII) on:
- Command Company
- 13th Company
- 14th Company
- 15th Company
- 16th Company

CI Battalion Complements on:
- Command
- Command Unit
- 1st Company
- 2nd Company
- Light Artillery Battery

At the end of January, at the oath ceremony, the Regiment had 5,000 men.

Losses

The confirmed dead of the 3rd Regiment Command number 3, but the list is certainly incomplete.

CI Battalion Complements Bersaglieri

It was incorporated in Alessandria in March 1944 with the task of recruiting and training troops for the Battalions of the 3rd Regiment; with the autonomy of the four Battalions, it changed its name to "I (CI) Battalion Complements - Coastal Defense", moving to Novi Ligure in the autumn of '44. With the return of the IV Battalion from the Apennine front, the Complement Battalion broke up. The department had the following structure:
- Command
- Command Unit
- 1st Bersaglieri Company
- 2nd Bersaglieri Company
- Infantry guns battery

I (LI) Coastal Defense Volunteer Bersaglieri Battalion

Located in defense of the city of Genoa with a garrison of permanent works and anti-aircraft and coastal defense tasks and of the small coastal convoys directed from Genoa to La Spezia, the First Battalion had garrisons in Nervi, Quinto, Pieve Ligure, near the breakwater, in Punta Vagno, Lido di Albaro, Quezzi, Battery Stella, Foce del Bisagno, etc., it was under the command of the "Meinhold" Group which guarded the so called "Great Genoa". The Battalion at the end of April 1945 did not surrender, but it was almost completely destroyed in furious fighting against the avant-garde of the 92nd "Buffalo" Division and against the partisans.

Commander of the Battalion was Lieutenant Colonel Garibaldo Giovan Battista.

Structure
- Command Company
- 1st Company
- 2nd Company
- 3rd Company
- 4th Company

The total strength of the Battalion included 35 officers, 98 non-commissioned officers and 660 soldiers.

Losses

The victims of the I Battalion amount to 11, but the list is certainly incomplete.

Weapons

Each platoon had 3 submachine guns, 1 Fiat 35 model machine gun and each company had an 81mm mortar platoon in its staff. Located in fixed locations around Genoa, the Battalion employed Breda 37 and Saint Etienne machine guns, cannons from 47/32 and 65/17. In some locations he also used 75/18 guns, 105/28 guns, Breda 20mm and 13.2mm machine guns.

II (XX) Coastal Defense Volunteer Bersaglieri Battalion

The 2nd Bersaglieri Coastal Defense Battalion was sent to Savona at the Legino barracks on February 20th, taking on, after a month of continuous training, the defense of the coast from Varazze to Albenga, under the jurisdiction of 34th German Infanteriedivision, with the following location of the departments: Command and Command Company in Savona, 5th Company from Varazze to Savona excluded, 6th Company from Savona to Pietra Ligure excluded, 7th Company from Pietra Ligure to Albenga excluded, 8th Company to Albenga. The Bersaglieri used fortified positions and bunkers, built for coastal defense, by the Todt Organization. During the period from the end of March to August, the Battalion suffered numerous air raids. The deployment of the II Coastal Defense Battalion was intended to allow the first intervention against possible landings, possible along the Ligurian coasts of the west, given the conformation of the land. Following the Allied landing in Provence, and the deployment of the "San Marco" Infantry Division of the Marina, between 2nd and 31st August the 2nd Battalion was transferred to the French border. The transfer was carried out on foot, while the materials were transported by wagons drawn by quadrupeds and the ammunition by barges by the sea. On 31 August the deployment of the Battalion was completed, with the following dislocation of the departments: Command and Command Company in Arma di Taggia, 5th Company from Monte Pozzo to Grimaldi on the French border, aggregated to the II Battalion of the 253th German Grenadier Regiment; 6th Company from Santo Stefano to San Lorenzo a Mare; 8th Company from Grimaldi to Bordighera, 7th Company between Ceriana and Taggia. The 5th Company was connected with German units on the right and with the 8th Company on the left. At that time, a new company was established, the 9th, with a reduced workforce of no more than 60/70, with the task of providing protection for communication routes and security against partisan groups. On the border the Bersaglieri came into contact with the French troops, in the area of Grammondo, and Americans, in the area of Grimaldi, with frequent clashes of patrols, skirmishes in the no man's land and fallen for mines. Numerous actions were carried out with the aim of capturing prisoners, to steal useful information for the defense of the sector. Towards the end of August and especially in September, partisan attacks on Bersaglieri positions intensified in conjunction with the allied operations in Provence. On 24th August, due to the betrayal of the Platoon Commander, the partisans entered the barracks and captured the entire Platoon of the 7th Company in Ceriana, 30 men with complete armament, including an 81 mm mortar1[6]. Only two Bersaglieri managed to escape prison after two weeks and return to the ward. On 17th September, two patrols fell into an ambush by partisans, suffering heavy losses. On September 25th, the 9th Company carried out a round-up in the Badalucco area and then went on to attack the same locality, site of a partisan command. The lack of strength of the forces, the lack of knowledge of the territory, the orography of the area that lent itself to ambushes, was exploited by the partisans who, hidden in the bush and among the rocks, destroyed the Company. The Bersaglieri had 28 fallen, including the Commander of the Company Lieutenant Inglese, many Bersaglieri were killed after the end of the battle. The intervention of other departments of Bersaglieri and German troops saved the 9th from total annihilation and allowed the recovery of the fallen and the wounded. On the 30th of the same month the garrison of Ceriana was again attacked, thanks to the betrayal of two German deserters, who facilitated the entry of the partisans in some defensive positions of the country. After the initial success, which entailed the capture of 10 Bersaglieri, the alarm and the prompt reaction of the garrison military, which, after a few hours of fighting, rejected the attack. The partisans then laid siege to the town, with the intention of dropping it[7]. A civilian

---

[6] It was Lieutenant De Sanctis who, with the complicity of Sergeant Baldo, handed over the Platoon to the partisans.

[7] On the occasion of the attack on the garrison of Ceriana, according to what a partisan wrote in a postwar publication, the partisans, to obtain the garrison's surrender, would have used some Bersaglieri captured as a shield to cover their advance, but this expedient did not it had the desired effect, as the defenders continued the fire making the attack fail. According to the testimony of veterans present at the battle, nothing happened as described in the book by the former partisan, as no overt attack was carried out in Ceriana. Instead, to resolve the impasse, the partisans sent a Bersagliere under Ceriana's command with a surrender request, under penalty of shooting all the prisoners in case of refusal. The Bersagliere Luigi Visconti, bearer of the partisan message, arrived

managed to arrive at the Battalion Command in Taggia, warning him of the situation that had arisen in Ceriana. Some Germans then left, with a 20mm machine gun and a 150mm howitzer towed by a truck, which undisturbed arrived in Ceriana, discovering that the partisans had now vanished. The Germans then proceeded to bombard with the howitzer of the town of Badalucco. After this fight, until the end of the garrison of the 7th Company in Ceriana, the partisans did not create more problems in the area and the 9th Company was immediately reconstituted and continued its surveillance work in the rear of the front. In mid-January a new line-up of the Battalion was prepared: the 6th Company plus a Platoon of the 7th was arranged by Montepozzo to Grimaldi, the 5th Company from Camporosso to Bordighera, with outposts to Grimaldi and Mortola, the 7th Company from Bordighera to Sanremo, the 8th Company from Grimaldi to Camporosso, the Command and Command Company in Ceriana, the 9th Company in Bajardo. In February, the 6th and 7th Company took over from the 5th, which was located between San Lorenzo al Mare and Santo Stefano al Mare, while the other Companies took sides between Imperia and Ponte San Luigi, controlling the Valle Argentina and the towns behind it. This deployment was maintained until April 23rd, 1945. Between 23rd and 2th4, the Battalion, obeying the folding order arrived from the Command of the 34th Infanteriedivision, concentrated all the companies on the Via Aurelia and began the retreat towards Piedmont in the direction of Ceva, leaving the 6th Company in the rear with tasks to support the German pioneers engaged in the destruction of some infrastructures. After having sustained some fighting with partisan forces in Sanremo on the 24th, along the route Ormea - Garessio - Ceva - Mondovì, completed between 26th and 29th April, the 6th Company was reunited with the Battalion at Savigliano. The second Battalion to complete, then continuing along the route followed by the 34th Infanteriedivision of General Lieb, reached Courgnè and finally Quagliuzzo, where, on the evening of May 3rd, it broke up.

Structure

- Command (in Savona, then Arma di Taggia)
  o Commander: Major Guido Castellari, then Major Antonio Mistretta, and finally Captain Pietro Borroni
  o Assistant Major: Lieutenant (later Captain) Giannone
  o Officers: Captain Giovanni Francoletti, Lieutenant Cuneo, Medical Lieutenant Ugo Broglia
- Command Company
  o Commander: Captain Giovanni Francoletti (then to the Supplies), then Lieutenant Salvatore Saved
- 5th Bersaglieri Company
  o Commander Captain Pietro Borroni, then Lieutenant Domenico Boni
  o Officers: Lieutenant Sergio Bandera, Lieutenant (then Lieutenant transferred to 9a) Buratti, Lieutenant Casalini, Lieutenant Mariotti, Lieutenant De Benedetti
- 6th Bersaglieri Company
  o Commander: Captain Josia
  o Officers: Lieutenant Spoto, Lieutenant Acerbi
- 7th Bersaglieri Company
  o Commander: Captain Italo Giannelli
  o Officers: Lieutenant Ezio Cecchini, Lieutenant Careers, Lieutenant De Sanctis, Lieutenant Perucchetti, Lieutenant Visintin
- 8th Bersaglieri Company
  o Commander: Lieutenant Ezio Cecchini, then Captain Ugo Bologna
  o Officers: Lieutenant Acerbi, Lieutenant Boni (then at the 5th), Lieutenant Trash, Lieutenant Longo
- 9th Bersaglieri Company

---

in front of the Commander of the Presidium, instead advocated the defense, and then brought to the partisans the message that the garrison would not surrender. The partisans withdrew, but when they arrived near Bajardo they shot 8 between graduates and Bersaglieri, the last to die was the Bersagliere Luigi Visconti.

o   Commander: Lieutenant Francesco Inglese, then Lieutenant Franco Buratti
o   Officers: Lieutenant Hood, Lieutenant Basket, Lieutenant Quartarolo

The strength of the II (XX) Coastal Defense Battalion, according to Pisanò, amounted to 36 officers, 141 non-commissioned officers and 740 troops; from the testimonies of some veterans the staff of the Battalion is instead calculated in about 400/500 soldiers, reduced to no more than 300 units towards the end of the conflict.

Weapons
The individual armament was typical of the Italian infantry: model '91 rifles, Breda 30 submachine guns, Beretta 34 pistols, some MABs, some weapons recovered from the partisans and allied launches. Each company was equipped with 2 81 mm mortars, 1 47/32 anti-tank piece and some machine guns.

Motor vehicles
There are no trucks supplied to the Battalion, wagons drawn by quadrupeds and mules were used to transport the materials.

Losses
The confirmed dead of the 2nd Bersaglieri Coastal Defense Battalion amount to 83, but the list is certainly incomplete. Of these fallen only 11 are to be charged to enemy fire, mainly due to the bombing, while 64 were killed by the partisans and the other 8 died due to accidents or diseases contracted due to war.

III (XXV) Coastal Defense Volunteer Bersaglieri Battalion

The Battalion was sent to Liguria where he took up the deployment from Varazze (GE) to Genoa, with the command of the Battalion at Bolzaneto (GE). The main activity of the department was to protect the coast in anti-embarkation, taking advantage of the bunkers and the prepared stations, operating under the "Meinhold" Group. In the late spring of 1944, a company, reinforced with elements of the XX Battalion, was sent to the island of Elba, in the summer another company was deployed in the area of Lavagna (GE). In April 1945 the Command and the Companies deployed in the west followed the forces exiting Genoa, the Company located in Lavagna joined the troops of the "Monterosa" Division. The Battalion ceased to exist between 28th and 30th April, after the surrender of the units to which it was attached. The first commander of the Battalion was Captain Paggiarino, then Captain Falomi Giuliano.

Structure
ï   Command Company
ï   9th Company
ï   10th Company
ï   11th Company
ï   12th Company

The total strength of the Battalion included 27 officers, 130 non-commissioned officers and 700 soldiers.

Losses
The confirmed dead of the 3rd Battalion add up to 7, but the list is certainly incomplete.

Weapons
Each platoon was equipped with 3 submachine guns, 1 machine gun and 1 81 mm mortar.

IV (XVIII) Coastal Defense Volunteer Bersaglieri Battalion

The Battalion was located in La Spezia, with the Companies positioned between Rapallo (GE) and La Spezia excluded, with anti-embarkation functions, a very delicate task due to the very jagged coastline and functionally depended on the Almers Brigade. With the arrival of the departments of the "Monterosa" Division, the Battalion was sent to the southern front, where it came into contact with the Americans and the partisans of the area, and later, in September 1944, it was transferred to the front of the Bolognese Apennines, where participated, inserted in the German deployment, to fierce fighting. The command was moved to Riolo di Vergato (BO). In November 1944 the Battalion went to rest in Noceto (PR), then returned to Tortona (AL) and ceased to exist in Alessandria on 28th April 1945. The first commander of the Battalion was Major Grana Piero, then Captain Bisio Giovanni, then Captain Grotti, and finally Captain Bisio Giovanni.

Structure
- Command Company
- 13th Company
- 14th Company
- 15th Company
- 16th Company

The total strength of the Battalion included 43 officers, 117 non-commissioned officers and 950 soldiers.

Losses
The confirmed dead of the 4th Battalion add up to 2, but the list is certainly incomplete.

Weapos
In the fixed positions on the coast the Battalion's units benefited from anti-aircraft gunners, anti-ship guns, heavy machine guns. The individual armament was of Italian origin: rifle and musket '91, Beretta pistols, Breda 30 submachine guns, MAB, Breda and Fiat machine guns.

1st Regiment "Bersaglieri di Marcia"

It consisted of the XXVI Bersaglieri Battalion, reconstituted in Turin between September and October of '43, and by the Bersaglieri Formation Battalion, reconstituted in Asti, with the intention of reconstituting the 4th Bersaglieri Regiment. The impossibility of reconstituting the 4th and the need to reinforce the Bersaglieri units of the newly formed "Italia" Division in training in Germany, caused the meeting of the two Battalions in Turin in the "1st March Regiment" on 1st April 1944, on 5th the Regiment's command was taken over by Lieutenant Colonel Tarsia. Once the two Battalions were reorganized, complete with men and weapons, the Regiment changed its name to "1st Bersaglieri Regiment of Formation Italia". At the end of May 1944, the Regiment, in stages, departed from Vercelli, where it had in the meantime moved, to reach the Heuberg training camp where the "Italia" Bersaglieri Division was being prepared by May 31st. The next day the regiment was dissolved, and his men became part of the various regiments of the Division, most of the XXVI Battalion merged into the IV Divisional Exploring Group.

Bersaglieri Volunteer Regiment "Luciano Manara"

After the departure to the eastern borders of the "Bersaglieri Battalion" "Mussolini" in mid-October 1943, at the Verona headquarters, where the volunteers continued to flow, the command of the "Luciano Manara" Bersaglieri Volunteer Regiment was established. In the last months of the year, at the Regiment's Command, the Regimental Command Company and the Depot were formed, where the volunteers formed the first temporary Companies. Thanks to the influx of volunteers, on February 20th, the 2nd Bersaglieri Battalion "Goffredo Mameli" was formed and, on May 20th, 1944, the 3rd Bersaglieri Battalion "Enrico Toti". The Regiment's Command remained stationed in Verona until the end of April 1945, then fell back to the Adige Valley where it was dissolved on the 30th. The Regiment was never used as an organic unit, but performed exclusively as a complementary training center and deposit for the Battalions located on the various fronts[8].

The first commander of the Regiment was Lieutenant Colonel Vittorio Facchini, subsequently Lieutenant Colonel Antonino Salvo, in temporary command.

Structure
i   Regimental Command Company

---

[8] In many publications reference is made to the 8th Bersaglieri Regiment, confirmed in the Mussolini barracks in Verona, but is historically inaccurate, in fact there was no continuity, if not ideal, between the Regiment, officially dissolved immediately after 8 September, and the unit that was formed around the few bersaglieri who remained in arms and were the base on which the "Luciano Manara" Regiment was established.

- Depot
- 1st Bersaglieri Volunteer Battalion "Benito Mussolini"[9]
- 2nd Bersaglieri Volunteer Battalion "Goffredo Mameli"
  - Command Platoon
  - 1st Company
  - 2nd Company
  - 3rd Assault Company
  - 4th Weapons Company
  - Carriages Unit
- 3rd "Enrico Toti" Bersaglieri Volunteer Battalion
  - Command Company
  - 1st Company
  - 2nd Company
  - 3rd Company

The "Mameli" Battalion had 53 officers, 2 chaplains officers, 80 non-commissioned officers, 78 graduates, 319 Bersaglieri and 6 Auxiliaries. The Battalion "Toti" instead had a total strength of 414 men, of which 34 were officers, 70 non-commissioned officers and 310 Bersaglieri.

Fallen

The proven victims of the "Mameli" amount to 70; the wounded, disabled and mutilated totaled 73, while the 3rd Battalion Volunteer Bersaglieri "Enrico Toti" had 1 ascertained dead, but the list is certainly incomplete.

Weapons

Mixed armament, Italian and German, then rifles '91 and Mauser 98K, machine guns Breda 37 and MG 42, panzerfaust mod. 30 and 60, MAB 38A. The "Mameli" Battalion had 12 81 mm CEMSA mortars and 10 Breda 37 machine guns in addition to some Walther Gewehr 41 and MP 38/40 rifles.

1st Bersaglieri Volunteer Battalion "Benito Mussolini" – XV Coastal Defense Battalion

Constituted immediately after 8th September, at the Depot of the 8th Bersaglieri Regiment in Verona, with the men remained in arms, thanks to the influx of numerous volunteers, on 19th September, under the command of Lieutenant Colonel Vittorio Facchini, it could appear at federal commissioner of the PFR of Verona. The initial core of the Battalion was composed of experienced non-commissioned officers and bersaglieri from the front of northern Africa, supplemented by officers, non-commissioned officers and military personnel of the "East Traded Center", for the rest by disbanded soldiers or former prisoners of the Germans who had joined the Facchini's appeal. To this initial nucleus it was added a substantial group of Veronese students. In October the Battalion moved to the Gorizia in two groups, on the 10th and 14th, moving to position in the middle Valle Isonzo and in the Valle Baccia. The initial contingent was gradually replaced by volunteers and recruits of the 1924 and 1925 classes, carried out its very important task of protecting against Slav infiltration for 19 very long months, without substitutions and with few complements to replace the losses. The Battalion ceased to exist on 30th April 1945 at the Caporetto hold.

The first commander of the Battalion was Lieutenant Colonel Vittorio Facchini, then Major Armando Cavalletti then Captain Ennio Mognaschi.

The Battalion "Mussolini" took several names in its brief history, initially "Volunteer Battalion Benito Mussolini of the Italian SS", then "I / 8 ° Bersaglieri", then "Bruno Mussolini", then "Stefano Rizzardi", then "XV Battalion Coastal Defense ", but for all it was always the Bersaglieri Battalion" Benito Mussolini ".

Employment area

The Battalion was sent to the Isonzo and Baccia valleys, positioning itself along the Gorizia - Piedicolle

---

9   Detailed information on the structure and staff of the "Mussolini" Bersaglieri Battalion can be found in the relevant paragraph.

railway line, from km 82 to km 109, with a series of detachments located in an area controlled by the enemy. It presided for a long period Saint Lucia of Isonzo and for five months Tolmino (today both in Slovenian territory). It resisted stupendously to the battles of annihilation of the end of June 1944 and of September of the same year, as it always reacted promptly to the actions of ambushes, attacks and guerrilla warfare, which the Slavic and Italian formations incorporated in them brought with continuity for all 19 months at the front. A characteristic of the Battalion was the "company fighting groups", very efficient for their mobility, which managed to inflict heavy losses on the enemy, represented by the IX Slovenian Korpus.

Deployment of the Battalion

Santa Lucia di Tolmino : Command – Command Company – Autodrappello
from Km 82 to Km 90 : 3rd Company
from Km 91 to Km 95 : 5th Company
from m 96 to Km 100 : 1st Company
from Km 101 to Km 105 : 4th Company
from Km 106 to Piedicolle : 2nd Company

Structure

- Battalion's Command
- Command Company
- 1st Company
- 2nd Company
- 3rd Company
- 4th Company
- 5th Company
- Autodrappello
- Administration Office
- Propaganda service

Staff

October '43 = 400/500 men
February '44 = 749 men, including 33 officers, 94 non-commissioned officers and 622 sharpshooters
June '44 = 1,299 men, including 39 officers, 98 non-commissioned officers and 1,062 bersaglieri
March '45 = 625 men, of which 30 are officers, 140 non-commissioned officers (105 official students) and 455 bersaglieri

It can be assumed that, therefore, the maximum strength of the Battalion, was reached in June '44, with about 1,350 men, equivalent to the consistency of three Cyclist Battalion in the Royal Army. In total the force passed in the Battalion was of about 2,300 men, of which 100 were officers. The presence in the ranks of the Battalion of Official Students is very high, around 150.

Losses

The fallen and missing in combat and in captivity of the Battalion are not less than 450, 25 of which are officers, while the number of injured, disabled and no longer fit for the service reaches 600.

Veichles

- 6 trucks Fiat 626
- 6 trailers
- 2 cars
- 1 ambulance
- motorcycles in unspecified numbers
- 1 maintenance workshop
- 1 self-propelled L40 of 47/32

Also available to the Battalion are about thirty mules, used for the most varied tasks.

Artillery

- 6 Breda 20 mm antiaircraft machine guns

- 6 Hotchkiss 25 mm antitank guns
- 1 Solothurn 20mm antitank rifle[10]
- 2 field cannons 75/27[11]

Armamento
- 20 81mm mortars
- 2 45mm Brixia mortars
- 40 8 mm Breda/Fiat machine guns
- 30 submachine guns *Bren*
- about 70 *Sten*[12]
- an unspecified number of model 91 rifles, Breda 30 submachine guns, MAB and MAS submachine guns, some flamethrowers, moreover never used.

2nd Bersaglieri Volunteer Battalion "Goffredo Mameli"[13]

On April 3rd, 1944, the Battalion was sent to Forlì and from there it settled on the Adriatic coast. On August 15th, while the unit was about to return to Verona, thanks to the intervention of the Duce, who had visited the ward a few days before, the 1st Assault Company was set up, with volunteers offered by the four Companies, which, after a very rapid two-week training at the 615th Lehrbataillon with German weapons, was sent in aggregate line to the 715th German Infantry Division on September 13th. The 1st Company had its baptism of fire on September 23rd and until the end of October, it was a succession of increasingly violent fights, with heavy losses inflicted and suffered (remember the battles of Monte Cucco, Monte Porrata, Monte Cristino, the area south of Castel Del Rio, Portonuovo Gazzolino, Monte Battaglia, Monte Cece, Monte Acuto, in the Val Santerno and in the Val Senio), with conquered quotas, lost and reconquered in the short space of even a few hours. At the end of this heavy operating cycle, the survivors of the 1st Company were sent to Verona for a period of rest and reorganization, of the 145 men who left very few were unharmed. Then the 2nd Company took over, and from November 25th to December 11th it was trained in the use of German weapons in Ortodonico, with a force of 140 men. From 12th December 1944 it was deployed at Riolo Bagni where it was halved in a short time. The survivors, no more than sixty, remained at the front until February 1945, while from November 1944 to March 1945 the personnel for the 3rd Company was trained in Bergamo, with a total force of 120 men. On March 18th, 1945, the 1st and 3rd Company of the "Mameli" 2nd Battalion left from Verona, the only ones remaining in the organic, to be incorporated, as complements, into the "Italia" Bersaglieri Division, deployed on the Garfagnana front. Arrived in Gaiano di Collecchio on the 27th, the 1st Company began escorting missions to Bersaglieri, arms and foodstuffs to Tuscany, as well as patrolling the Fornovo-Parma railway and preventing acts of sabotage on the bridge over the Taro, which connects Cisa with the Medesano-Noceto-Fidenza road. On 4th April two Plotons were sent to Villafranca in Lunigiana with escort duties for some batteries, then, after clashes with the partisans in Berceto and Monzone, they reached Gragnola, then moved to Viano, where on 22nd April they clashed with the allied troops . When the folding order arrived, the Bersaglieri of the 1st Company headed towards Fivizzano but, since this was already in enemy hands, they diverted to Fornovo, reached on April 27th,

---

10 According to one veteran, the Solothurn rifles were 2 and not 1, while according to other sources, it was only one, which was transferred from one company to another in 1944.

11 The 75/27 guns were found on the square of Santa Lucia, certainly they were used in a retaliatory action after being ambushed by Captain Mori, on this occasion some villages were bombed around S. Lucia causing some civilian deaths. There is no news of other actions.

12 The Sten and the Bren were recovered thanks to some allied airplanes intercepted by the Bersaglieri towards the end of 1944.

13 The "Mameli" Battalion was undoubtedly one of the most decorated units of the Army of the R.S.I., also in consideration of the fact that it was never used in an organic way, but only at the level of company. In total: 6 Silver Medals for Military Valor, 16 Bronze Medals for Military Valor, 5 War Crosses for Military Valor, 3 Promotions for War Merits, 2 Eisernes Kreuz, 1st Class, 42 Eisernes Kreuz, 2nd Class, 32 Infantry Assault Badges (Infanterie Sturm-Abzeichen).

where they were employed in the Collecchio area and then in Medesano. On the 28th, Lieutenant Dani, commander of the Company, dissolved the unit in Fellegara di Medesano. The 3rd Company was seconded to Sala Baganza where it carried out tasks of garrison on the Taro and provided for the escort of a convoy to Pontremoli. On April 26th, it fell back to Parma and then to Garda where it broke up. Commander of the Battalion was Major Leonardo Vannata. The Combat Group incorporated into the "Italy" Division was at the command of Captain Saverio Martucci.

3rd Volunteers Battalion Bersaglieri "Enrico Toti"

It was established on May 20, 1944 in Verona, always remained in the city, and at the end of April 1945 it fell back to Val d'Adige in the direction of Trento. It disbanded before reaching the city.
Commander of the Battalion was Major Sandro Bonamici.

1st Company "Bersaglieri del Mincio" – Raggruppamento "Cacciatori degli Appennini"

One of the main problems that emerged during the fight against the guerrilla war against partisans in Yugoslavia was the complete absence of Regio Esercito units specifically trained for this task. The struggle against the partisans in Italy was addressed by the Army General Staff of R.S.I. making use of this nefarious experience, creating in the spring - summer of 1944 two unitts with specific training for the partisan struggle, the "Hunter of the Apennines" ("Cacciatori degli Appennini") group and the Anti Partisan Group (Raggruppamento Anti Partigiani), unit with the staff and the equipment of a light Brigade, both located in Piedmont.
The "Bersaglieri del Mincio" Company was set up with enlisted elements in Mantua and it was part of the Exploring Group of the "Cacciatori degli Appennini".
Commanded by Lieutenant Bruno Gallese, it reached a maximum staff of 130 Bersaglieri.

1st Battalion Arditi Bersaglieri – Raggruppamento Anti Partigiani

The establishment of Arditi Battalions to be included in the R.A.P. dates back to July 1944, when the creation of three Battalions was planned to be specifically trained for anti-partisan's use, with about 2,000 men strong. Between July and November these units were actually set up, in fact one was formed more than expected. The 1st Battalion Arditi Bersaglieri, initially called 1st Controguerriglia Battalion, was established in Brescia on 25th July 1944. Also known as "Mazzini" Battalion, it later changed its name to the official one of 1st Arditi Bersaglieri Battalion; it was commanded by Major Antonio Pacinotti, who was succeeded by the Major General Staff Filippo Galamini, and it was divided into:
- Command Company
- 1st Bersaglieri Company
- 2nd Bersaglieri Company
- 3rd Bersaglieri Company

The Command Company also had an Healthcare Team equipped with four ambulances. The unit had approximately 590 men; the Battalion's list of honor includes 4 Silver Medals for Military Valor and 8 Bronze. In autumn 1944 it was engaged in offensive episodes on Biella, then in Val d'Aosta and finally in Val Pellice. The Battalion was disbanded in January 1945 and had a total of 5 known fallen (according to other sources 13 known fallen and 85 unknown).

Bersaglieri – Alpini Mixed Company

It was established in Perugia with personnel coming from Bersaglieri and Alpini, present in the Umbrian city, in October 1943, in February 1944 it took its oath of fidelity to the Italian Social Reppublic. The Company's strength included 6 officers, 14 non-commissioned officers and 97 soldiers.

Other units

1st Battalion of Italian Volunteer "Ettore Muti"

In Florence, a large number of volunteers all from the dissolved 5th Bersaglieri Regiment set up a unit on September 14th, 1943, a few days after the Armistice, at the former headquarters of the Italian "Gioventù del Littorio", which was configured as a Battalion on two Companies. The "Muti" Battalion was initially used for the recovery of weapons and materials abandoned in the city and in the surrounding areas by the Royal Army, and subsequently participated throughout the province in large-scale police operations throughout the winter of 1943 - '44. In August 1944 the Battalion was transferred to Bologna under the command of the 202nd Regional Military Command, being always employed in tasks of defense and repression. After a brief transfer to Schio, in the autumn the Command and one Company were moved to Verona, while the other Company was in Garda. On April 28th, 1945 the "Muti" Battalion broke up, after meeting a few days earlier in Verona. Captain Giuseppe Bindi was the commander of the Battalion, which had a total force of 256 soldiers and complained at least 22 fallen (of which 15 were unknown).

The "Muti" Battalion consisted of:
ï   Command
ï   1st Company
ï   2nd Company

Although it was not officially a Bersaglieri department, the unit kept the insignia of the Corp, to signal the targeting of its volunteers. In fact, on the cap was carried a frieze composed of a flaming Bersaglieri grenade, with two crossed lictor beams. The insignia were initially rectangular, loaded with a crimson flame with two points. Subsequently the simple flames were adopted with three points, always of crimson color, with silver skulls.

Compagnia Bersaglieri "Curzio Casalecchi" – Legione Autonoma Mobile "Ettore Muti"

The Bersaglieri Company of the "Muti" Legion (a department formally belonging to the Republican Police, but de facto autonomous, hardly engaged in anti-partisan repression) was established on 3rd January 1945. The Company was named after Lieutenant Curzio Casalecchi of the "Domenico Savino" Company of the " Muti", was killed by the partisans on 2nf October 1944, after being captured during an attack carried to the checkpoint he commanded on the outskirts of Borgosesia. The Bersaglieri Company was dislocated in Valsesia in the so called "Safety Zone 20", initially right inside the city of Borgosesia, then going to support the "Figini" Company in Varallo Sesia. At the end of the conflict it retreated to Milan, joined the column of the Legion "Muti" which merged with Como on April 26, where it dissolved on April 28th. Commander of the "Curzio Casalecchi" Company was Captain Giorgio Barigazzi, who was replaced by Lieutenant Luigi Colombo in March 1945.

"Fulmine" Battalion – "Decima" Division

The "Fulmine" Battalion was an atypical component of Borghese's Xª MAS, since it was set up with personnel from the dissolved Royal Army, mainly from the Bersaglieri (especially the 11th Regiment and the 31st Tank Regiment), in the intentions of its founder, the Lieutenant Colonel Luigi Carallo, it should have belonged to the specialty of the Bersaglieri, from whom he himself came. Initially also the name of the Battalion was just "Bersagliere", but later it took the name of "Lightning", in honor of the destroyer of the Regia Marina sunk on June 13th 1941. The "Fulmine" was structured on Company Command and three Companies, the 3rd composed only of Italian volunteers from France, and it was operational from the summer of 1944 until its dissolution on 30th April in Schio.

A perennial memory of the original soul that animated Lieutenant Colonel Carallo, a helmet was represented with the typical black feather of the Bersaglieri both on the fighting flame and on the breast badge of the Battalion. The 1st Company also supplied a certain number of Bicycles, a symbol of the Bersaglieri since the beginning of the 20th century.

▲ Heuberg: Group of Bersaglieri of the "Italia" Division during training for interview with German instructors (Viziano)

▼ In the Heuberg training camp the Bersaglieri of the "Italia" Division gained confidence even with German weapons, such as these machine gunners with an MG42 (Viziano)

▲ Hand to hand combat training of the Bersaglieri of the "Italy" Division (Viziano)

▼ Demonstration of "Italia" in Heuberg in the presence of General Mainardi, commander of the Division (Viziano)

▲ The soldiers of the Division set off to honor the local monument that commemorates the fallen Germans of the Great War (Viziano)
▼ Deposition of floral wreaths at the First Word War memorial of Heuberg (Viziano)

▲ Training of the Bersaglieri of the "Italia" Division in the use of portable radios (Viziano)

▼ Telephoners' platoon during training in Heuberg: note the use of German material (Viziano)

▲ Bersagliere in training in the field of Heuberg (Viziano)

▲ Front of the "Gothic": the Bersaglieri of the "Italia" Division enter the line (Viziano)

▼ Close up of a shelter for the Bersaglieri of the "Italia" Division on the "Gothic" Line (Viziano)

▲ Bersaglieri of the "Italia" Division in a hole armed with a 81mm mortar (Viziano)

▼ Observatory of the "Italia" Division at Le Tese in Garfagnana (Viziano)

▲ Bersaglieri of the 3rd Battalion / 1st Regiment of the "Italia" Division at Le Tese (Viziano)

▼ Gunners of the 2nd Regiment in the rear of the "Gothic", note the MG42 and the huge supply of ammunition carried by the two servants (Viziano)

▲ Bersaglieri of the Division "Italia" with 81mm mortar, intent on stripping the grenades (Viziano)

▲ A moment of pause for these Bersaglieri of the 2nd Regiment on the "Gothic" Line (Viziano)

▼ Machine-gun nest of the 3rd Battalion / 1st Regiment of "Italy in Le Tese in Garfagnana (Viziano)

▲ Communication between the positions of the "Italy" Division, often distant from each other, on the "Gothic" front was vital. Line guard is repairing a telephone cable (Viziano)

▼ Intense close-up of a young Bersagliere of the 2nd Regiment. On the helmet bears the new frieze, representing a republican eagle, which was to be adopted on all military helmets of the Republican National Army, replacing the royal specialty friezes (Viziano)

▲ Poster inciting enrollment in the 1st Bersaglieri Division "Italia" (Crippa)

▲ Changing of the guard between two Bersaglieri of the "Italia" Division in Garfagnana (Viziano)

▲ Bersaglieri of the "Italia" Division transport ammunition to the front line, wearing makeshift camouflage garments, to hide on the snowy ground. The supply of weapons and ammunition was made difficult by adverse weather conditions (Viziano)

▲ Bersaglieri patrol of the "Italia" Division, on patrol on the front of the "Gothic" Line. The soldier in the foreground wears an Italian curtain, facing the inside, to make himself less visible in the snow (Viziano)

▲ Bersaglieri of the "Italia" supply division supervise the ammunition boxes (Viziano)

▼ A German IG18 75/10 howitzer is placed in position by the servants on the "Gothic" Line (Viziano)

▲ Bersagliere of the "Italia" Division assigned to a German IG18 howitzer 75/10 (Viziano).

▲ In January 1945 the Duce visited the departments of the "Italy" Division deployed along the Gothic Line (Viziano)

▼ Mussolini gets out of his car, surrounded by officers from the Division (Viziano)

▲ The Duce reviews the Bersaglieri, under a heavy snowfall. Behind him, on the left, his inseparable orderly, Pietro Carradori (Viziano)

▼ Mussolini visiting the positions of the "Italy" Division on the "Gothic" (Viziano)

▲ Bersaglieri of the II Exploring Group of the "Littorio" Division (Cucut)

▼ Ceremony in the presence of war widows in the province of Cuneo. The Bersaglieri of the Exploring Group of the "Littorio" Division are present (Cucut)

▲ The pennant of the II Exploring Group of the "Littorio" Division during a Holy Mass, presided over by soldiers, by young people from the National Opera Balilla and the White Flames, in a small town in the Cuneo area (Cucut)

▼ In this photograph taken during the same manifestation of the previous image it is possible to clearly see the other side of the pennant of the II Exploring Group of the "Littorio" Division, which bears the words "BERSAGLIERI ESPLORATORI LITTORIO" (Cucut)

▲ Machine-gunner of the Exploring Group "Cadelo" of the "Monterosa" Division observes the enemy movements from his position in Garfagnana (Viziano)

▼ Pitch of a German howitzer IG18 of 75/10 of the "Cadelo" in Garfagnana (Archivio Associazione Divisione Monterosa)

▲ Bersaglieri of the "Cadelo" Group in Piazza al Serchio in February 1945, to note the extremely heterogeneous clothing of the military (Archivio Associazione Divisione Monterosa)

▲ Officers of the "Cadelo" Group at Quota 1029 in Garfagnana (Archivio Associazione Divisione Monterosa)

▲ Major Cadelo, commander of the Exploration Group of the "Monterosa" Division (Archivio Associazione Divisione Monterosa)

▲ Lieutenant Colonel Andolfato of the "Cadelo" Exploration Group of the "Monterosa" Division in conversation with the Lieutenants Valparaiso, Capponi and Giovenc and some German officers (Viziano)

▼ Group photo of Bersaglieri of the "Cadelo" Group of the "Monterosa" Division in Terrarossa (GE) (Archivio Associazione Divisione Monterosa)

▲ Bersaglieri of the 3rd "Natisone" Battalion of the "Tagliamento" Regiment in Valle d'Isonzo (Archivio Reduci Reggimento "Tagliamento")

▼Group of Bersaglieri of the 8th Company of "Natisone" in Ronzina on 17 August 1944. The clothing is very heterogeneous (you can see both khaki, camouflage, jackets, fez, sachets) and the armament I suggest that the photo was taken at the end of a territorial control operation (Archivio Reduci Reggimento "Tagliamento")

▲ Fortified defensive position of the "Natisone" in the Baccia Valley (Archivio Reduci Reggimento "Tagliamento")

▲ Observation post and guardhouse of the "Natisone" Battalion, reinforced by a FIAT model 35 machine gun (Archivio Reduci Reggimento "Tagliamento")

▲ Bersaglieri of the 3rd "Natisone" Battalion of the "Tagliamento" Regiment (including a chaplain) in Santa Lucia d'Isonzo (Archivio Reduci Reggimento "Tagliamento")

▼ Bersaglieri of the "Natisone" of the "Tagliamento" Regiment attend Mass at the camp at Chiesa San Giorgio in the autumn of 1944 (Archivio Reduci Reggimento "Tagliamento")

▲ Bersaglieri motociclisti of the III Battalion "Natisone" a Ronzina (Archivio Reduci Reggimento "Tagliamento")

▲ Italian 47/32 anti-tank gun of the 8th Company of "Natisone" Battalion (Archivio Reduci Reggimento "Tagliamento")

▼ Platoon of Bersaglieri of the 3rd Bersaglieri Regiment being trained in Tortona on 2 February 1944 (Malfettani)

▲ Bersaglieri of the 3rd Regiment being trained in Tortona with a 47 mm Italian anti-tank gun. Many of them are armed with Lebel rifles of 8 mm of prey of war (Malfettani)

▼ Coastal position of the Bersaglieri of a Coastal Defense Battalion in Liguria (Cucut)

▲ The young Bersagliere volunteer Franco Bruno of the 3rd Bersaglieri Regiment. The soldier wears the Italian camouflage tent, on which he has pinned the beautiful badge of university volunteers of the 5th Company of the II Battalion (Malfettani)

▲ Studio photo of a Bersagliere of the 5th Company of the 2nd Battalion of the 3rd Bersaglieri Regiment, composed of university volunteers (you can see the beautiful badge applied on the pocket of the jacket). The soldier wears a wind jacket, on which are sewn the major corporal gallons, bearing a metallic skull. At the collar the flames of the Bersaglieri bear the sword of the Social Republic (Chionetti)

▲ Lieutenant Colonel Giovan Battista Gariboldo, commander of the 1st Bersaglieri Defense Defense Battalion talking to some of his men (Scarone)

▼ The Head of the Province of Genoa Carlo Emanuele Basile and General Renzo Butti review the Bersaglieri of the 1st Coastal Defense Battalion, deployed in Piazza della Vittoria on 12th March 1944 (Malfettani)

▲ Republican military during a ceremony in the Ligurian capital. These are Bersaglieri of the 1st Battalion of the 3rd Regiment and of young women of the White Flames. The Bersagliere in the foreground still bears the stars on the flames with two crimson spikes, typical of the specialty (Scarone)

▲ Bersaglieri platoon of the 1st Battalion of the 3rd Bersaglieri Regiment in Piazza della Vittoria in Genoa. The Battalion was initially called LI Battaglione Bersaglieri (Scarone)

▼ Bersaglieri of the Coastal Defense Battalion refuel with the Auxiliaries of O.N.D. after training for a patriotic demonstration in Genoa in March 1944. The soldiers have camouflaged helmets (Malfettani)

▲ The comfort items are distributed by a "mobile cellar" to the Bersaglieri of the I Battalion (Malfettani)
▼ An Ausiliaria offers drinks to a Bersagliere of the 1st Coastal Defense Battalion (Malfettani)

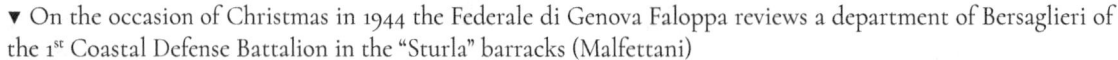

▲ The pace of the race remained an essential feature even during the R.S.I.: in this photo we see the Bersaglieri of the 1st Battalion Bersaglieri Volunteer Coastal Defense during a demonstration in Genoa (Scarone)

▼ On the occasion of Christmas in 1944 the Federale di Genova Faloppa reviews a department of Bersaglieri of the 1st Coastal Defense Battalion in the "Sturla" barracks (Malfettani)

▲ Bersagliere of the 2nd Battalion Bersaglieri Volunteer Coastal Defense in Porto Maurizio (IM). The soldier wears an out of order camouflage jacket, made with Italian camouflage fabric M1929 (Scarone)

▲ Some girls bring small gifts to Bersaglieri of the 1st Coastal Defense Battalion in the "Sturla" barracks in Genoa, on the same occasion as the previous photograph. The soldiers adopted, following the custom of the Germanic Armed Forces, the tricolor shield on the left side of the helmet, which appears camouflaged (Malfettani)

▼ Bersaglieri of the 2nd Battalion of the 3rd Bersaglieri Regiment in the province of Imperia (Scarone)

▲ Group of Officers of the 2nd Bersaglieri Battalion of the 3rd Bersaglieri Regiment in barracks (Scarone)

▼ Military ceremony in Ceriana (IM) in the presence of Fra 'Ginepro from Pompeiana, with the participation of a group of Bersaglieri of the II Coastal Defense Battalion with the fanfare. Fra 'Ginepro, a Capuchin friar, was a journalist, preacher, writer, poet, military chaplain and ardent supporter of the fascist cause. (Scarone)

▲ Bersaglieri of the II Coastal Defense Battalion participate in a patriotic ceremony in Sanremo in October 1944 (Pisanò)

▲ View of the II Bersaglieri Battalion on the Ligurian coast (Arena)

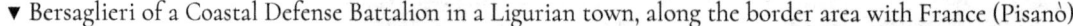
▲ Mopping operation conducted by soldiers of the II Coastal Defense Battalion on the hills of San Remo (Pisanò)

▼ Bersaglieri of a Coastal Defense Battalion in a Ligurian town, along the border area with France (Pisanò)

▲ Holy Christmas 1944 on the heights of Sanremo: Fra' Ginepro among the Bersaglieri of the II Coastal Defense Battalion, in hand has the "Child of the Frontier". The clothing of the military is very heterogeneous, some Bersaglieri also wear garments made of Italian camouflage fabric M1929 (Malfettani)

▼ Bersaglieri volunteers of the battalion "Mussolini": interesting the use of skulls on the crimson flames (Pisanò)

▲ The highly decorated Lieutenant Colonel Vittorio Facchini, first commander of the Bersaglieri Volunteer Battalion "Mussolini". Note that the officer carries the badge of specialty of the Submarinists of the Regia Marina to his chest (Crippa)

▲ The Bersaglieri of the "Mussolini" leaving for the Julian front in the courtyard of the barracks of the 8th Bersaglieri Regiment in Verona. The officer in the back is the commander Lieutenant Colonel Vittorio Facchini (Crippa)

▼ A group of Bersaglieri from the "Mussolini" parade in Piazza delle Erbe in Verona, before leaving for the Julian front with the fanfare of the department in the strictest tradition of the feathered infantrymen (Pisanò)

▲ Lieutenant Colonel Facchini on the same occasion of the previous image: the frieze of the Bersaglieri of the cap is interesting, which in the center of the rod, instead of having the number of the Regiment to which it belongs, shows off a skull (Crippa).

▲ A very young machine-gunner of the "Mussolini", he still bears the stars of the Royal Army on the crimson flames, which is quite common among the soldiers of the department, who left for the front before the distribution of the "gladio" and the republican friezes (Pisanò)

▼ Bersagliere of the "Mussolini" Battalion on patrol at high altitude. The soldier wears the typical uniform distributed to the military of the department: on the waterproof jacket, already used by the Royal Army, he wears a metallic skull, a very common symbol among the Bersaglieri of the Battalion (Viziano)

▲ Interior of a guard station of the XV Coastal Defense Battalion "Mussolini (Viziano)

▼ Small group of Bersaglieri of the "Mussolini" in front of their own fort. The Battalion established itself with many small fortified garrisons on a vast area, to cover the territory from slave infiltrations (Viziano)

▲ The armament of the "Mussolini" Battalion was enriched over the months by English weapons stolen by the Bersaglieri from the materials of the allied airplanes destined for the Yugoslav partisans, as in the case of this Bren submachine gun (Viziano)

▼ The "Mussolini" was supplied with at least one Solothurn counter-tank rifle (Viziano)

▲ Propaganda photo in which partially appears the 47/32 self-propelled used by the "Mussolini" Battalion (Francesconi)

▼ Bersaglieri of the "Mussolini" under enemy fire (Viziano)

▲ The pennant of the Arditi Plotone of the 1st Company of the Battalion "Mussolini" in Coritenza (Francesconi)

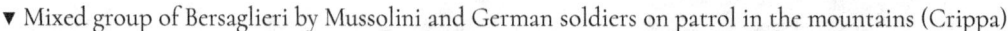

▲ The pennant of the Bersaglieri Volunteer Battalion "Benito Mussolini" during a ceremony in Santa Lucia d'Isonzo, October 1944 (Francesconi)

▼ Mixed group of Bersaglieri by Mussolini and German soldiers on patrol in the mountains (Crippa)

▲ Mortarists of the "Mussolini" Battalion in action in the winter of 1944 - '45 (Pisanò)

▼ Bersaglieri of the "Mussolini" observe the movements of the Slavic partisans during a counter-insurgency operation in March 1944 (Crippa)

▲ Photograph taken during a pause in the operation of the previous image (Crippa)

▲ Position defended by a 20 mm Breda machine gun of the "Mussolini" Battalion (Pisanò)
▼ Italian-German mixed station on the Gorizia-Piedicolle railway, held by Bersaglieri of the "Mussolini", who proudly raised a tricolor (Pisanò)

▲ A group of young Bersaglieri volunteers from the "Mussolini" in Val Baccia while singing a song (Pisanò)
▼ Bersaglieri of the 3rd Company of the "Mameli" Battalion in the Verona barracks (Liazza)

▲ The Lieutenant Gallerati commander of the 3rd Company of the Battalion "Mameli" (Liazza)

▲ Lieutenant Dani, commander of the 1st Company of the "Mameli" Battalion (Liazza)

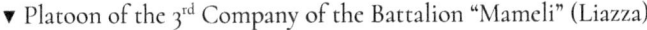
▲ Bersaglieri of the 1st Company of the "Mameli" Battalion moving to the Senio Valley (Liazza)

▼ Platoon of the 3rd Company of the Battalion "Mameli" (Liazza)

▲ Officers and non-commissioned officers of the 3rd Company of the "Mameli" Battalion (Liazza)

▲ Machine-gunners of the "Mameli" (Arena)

▼ Anti – landing training on the Adriatic coast of Bersaglieri of the "Mameli" battalion (Arena).

▲ The summer clothing of these Bersaglieri of the "Mameli" shows how the most disparate items of clothing were used homogeneously: shorts in khaki cloth, black shirts, khaki shirts, boots, leather leggings (Cucut).

▲ The fanfare and a picket of the "Mameli" Battalion deployed in the Verona barracks (Liazza)

▼ Young volunteers of the "Mameli" Battalion: only the officer regularly wears the gladius on the crimson flames, the troop men all still have the royal stars (Crippa)

▲ Machine-gun position of the "Mameli" Battalion during a territorial control operation in Emilia-Romagna in July 1944 (Crippa)

▼ Machine-gunner of the "Mameli" Battalion armed with a German machine-gun MG 42 (Crippa)

▲ Group of Bersaglieri of the "Enrico Toti" Battalion in the barracks of the 8th Regiment in Verona in June 1944 (Pisanò)
▼ Recruitment of volunteer Bersaglieri for the Bersaglieri Company "Mincio" of the "Cacciatori degli Appennini (Pisanò)

▲ The first volunteers, almost all from Mantua, are immediately framed to begin training (Pisanò)

▼ Training of the Bersaglieri of the "Mincio" Company (Pisanò)

▲ The bicycle was an irreplaceable companion also for the Bersaglieri of the R.S.I. (Crippa)

▼ Bersaglieri of the Constitution Center Great Units of Vercelli parade through the streets of the city in April 1944. The official at the center of the photograph is General Filippo Diamanti, commander of the Center (Pisanò)

▲ Military of the "Muti" Battalion of Florence receive gifts from the population at the end of an event organized in support of the Republican Armed Forces (Pisanò)

▼ Although the "Muti" Battalion was not actually classified as a Bersaglieri ward, it kept evident symbologies on its uniforms that can be traced back to the feathered infantry. In the uniform of the soldier in the foreground, the cap frieze almost identical to that of the Bersaglieri and the flames with two crimson spikes, initially under black pannus can be seen very well (Pisanò)

BIBLIOGRAPHY

Books and publications

- AA.VV., "*Soldati e Battaglie della Seconda Guerra Mondiale*", Hobby & Work Italiana Editrice, Bresso (MI), 1999.
- Arena Nino, "*R.S.I. – Forze Armate della Repubblica Sociale – La guerra in Italia – 1943 – 1944 – 1945*", Ermanno Albertelli Editore, Parma, 2002.
- Corbatti Sergio, Nava Marco, "*Come il diamante*", Laran Editions, Bruxelles, 2008.
- Crippa Paolo, "*I mezzi corazzati italiani della Guerra Civile 43- 45*", Mattioli 1885, Fidenza (PR), 2015.
- Crippa Paolo, "*I Reparti Corazzati della Repubblica Sociale Italiana 1943 -1945*", Marvia Edizioni, Voghera (PV), 2006.
- Cucut Carlo, "*Le Forze Armate della R.S.I. 1943 – 1945 – Forze di terra*", G.M.T., Trento, 2005.
- Cucut Carlo, Bobbio Roberto, "*Attilio Viziano – Ricordi di un corrispondente di guerra*", Marvia Edizioni, Voghera (PV), 2008.
- Kuchler Hein, "*Fregi mostrine distintivi della RSI*", Intergest, Milano, 1974.
- Pisanò Giorgio, "*Gli ultimi in grigioverde*", Edizioni F.P.E., Milano, 1967.
- Pisanò Giorgio, "*Storia della Guerra Civile in Italia*", Edizioni F.P.E., Milano, 1967.
- Rocco Giuseppe, "*Con l'Onore per l'Onore – L'organizzazione militare della R.S.I. sul finire della Seconda Guerra Mondiale*", Greco & Greco Editori s.r.l., Milano, 1998.
- Sparacino Franco, "*Distintivi e medaglie della R.S.I.*" Editrice Militare Italiana, Milano, 1983.

Magazines

- Scalpelli Adolfo, "*La formazione delle forze armate di Salò attraverso i documenti dello Stato Maggiore della R.S.I.*" in "*Il movimento di liberazione in Italia*" numbersi 72 e 73, 1963.
- "*Acta*", various numbers, Fondazione della R.S.I. - Istituto Storico, Terranuova Bracciolini (AR).
- "*Uniformi ed armi*", various numbers, Ermanno Albertelli Editore, Parma.